WELCOME TO YOKOSUKA

A Practical Guide on
How to PCS to Yokosuka, Japan

WELCOME TO YOKOSUKA
Copyright © 2018 by Ciara Skiles

ISBN-13: 978-1975871147
ISBN-10: 1-9758-7114-6

WELCOME TO YOKOSUKA

A Practical Guide on
How to PCS to Yokosuka, Japan

CIARA SKILES

DEDICATION

I'd like to dedicate this book to my loving and supportive husband, Elliott. I am so grateful to have you as my partner and teammate in this crazy life. It is truly a gift to have someone by my side who loves me entirely, challenges me to be my best self and encourages all of my big dreams and aspirations. You are so much more than I could have ever dreamed of. I love you and will keep you forever.

ACKNOWLEDGEMENTS

I would like to thank all the spouses and services members who contributed support and advice to help make this book a reality. It is overwhelming how much my "village" encouraged me in this endeavor. However, I must give a special thank you to Karla Langham, for being one of my biggest cheerleaders. The countless hours spent in her home, not only discussing this book but all the ways we can thrive in this lifestyle, have been invaluable. I love you, sweet friend. Thank you for all the kindness, hospitality and pep talks. They will never be forgotten.

TABLE OF CONTENTS

1. PREFACE

So you've just received the word you're going to Yokosuka, Japan... now what?

How are you feeling? Excited? Nervous? Happy? Overwhelmed? Maybe a little bit of all of those combined? It's totally normal to experience a range of emotions when you receive orders anywhere, let alone to an OCONUS, or overseas, duty station. While the prospect of living overseas can be exciting, the process of moving can be daunting, and filled with questions like "how will I get there," "how long will it take my things to arrive," "what should I take with me or leave in storage?"

The book is structured to help answer your questions, and break down the necessary tasks for your move based on the typical PCS timeline, which we will get into in just a bit. I will do my best to list the "to do's" in order of priority, as well as in an order that makes the most sense logistically. However, these are guidelines meant to be a starting point to help you feel less overwhelmed. I encourage you to read everything through completely when you find out you're moving. This way, you will have an understanding of what the process looks like from beginning to end, and also be able to then compartmentalize your tasks based on where you are in the process.

Here are the milestones I use to break down the PCS process:

- Verbal Orders And Letter Of Intent Hard Copy Orders
- 30-60 Days From Moving Day Week Of The Move
- Arriving
- The First Two Weeks

While the tools and resources I reference in this book are meant to be helpful, again, they are guidelines. Policies are subject to change at any time, so I encourage you to seek out authoritative information which is best found through resources like Military OneSource, your gaining command and/or your Ombudsman or branch equivalent.

My goal with this book is to help anyone moving to Yokosuka, Japan keep their sanity intact by using streamlined lists and timelines, so you can effectively prepare and execute your PCS without the hassle of sifting through countless Facebook or blog posts for vital information.

2. VERBAL ORDERS & LETTER OF INTENT

So your service member has just received verbal orders, and a letter of intent stating that you're slated for an accompanied tour to Yokosuka, Japan. As a spouse, your mind is probably going in a million different directions. If you're a seasoned mil spouse, and or have done an OCONUS move before, you're most likely already making a mental checklist of things that need to be done. If this is your first move, you're probably thinking "where do I start?" The starting point I recommend is to not panic. Take heart in the fact that you're not the first family that has made this move, and you will not be the last. The fact that you are reading this book means that you are being proactive, which is already a step in the right direction.

While there are many things you cannot do without hard copy orders, there are preparations that can and *should* be made as soon as you receive verbal orders and a letter of intent. So let's jump into some actionable steps that you can take of before those hard orders arrive.

Here is your checklist of to do's in order of importance, with more detailed explanations of what each thing is, and why you need it below:

1. Overseas screening
2. Pet requirements
3. PCS binder
4. No Fee Passports
5. Budget
6. Pack out prep

Overseas Suitability Screening

**Forms DD2807 1300/1

The overseas screening process is in place to ensure that the military isn't sending you to a duty station that won't be able to support the medical needs of your family. A screening must be done for each OCONUS duty station, meaning if you are already OCONUS going to another OCONUS location, you will still be required to complete one for each accompanying dependent.

The document itself is fairly straightforward. However, depending on how prepared you are, the process can take anywhere from a single day, to several weeks. I have experienced both ends of the spectrum. Best way to avoid a drawn-out process is to have certain records and documents with you when you head to the office that handles overseas screenings. Here is a rough step by step of what you will need to do:

1. Go to the military hospital closest to you that handles the overseas screening process to get separate packets for all dependents planning on PCSing with you. Ask them to walk you through each part of the process and what documents you'll need.

2. Make any necessary doctor and/or dentist appointments for each dependent.

3. At the doctor's appointment, they will be checking to make sure you do not have any major health concerns and are up to date on vaccinations. If you are not, they will advise you on what you'll need, as well as what vaccines are required for your upcoming move. If you have vaccination records, bring them. If you have other health issues, have those records on hand to be able to show the physician as well. It is better to be prepared with more documentation, than not enough. No one likes having to make a separate appointment, and go back if you're missing something.

4. For the dentist portion of the screening, it will go one of two ways.

    1. If you've recently been seen by a military dentist, they will generally just review your records that are on file, sign your screening form and send you on your way saying that you are A-OK. You may not even have to make an appointment. Best thing to do is to call ahead and ask what the protocol is. Every facility is a bit different.

2. If you usually see a nonmilitary dentist, you will need to make an appointment with the military dentist on base. Generally, they will take x-rays and do a basic exam to ensure you don't have any immediate needs. If you've recently been to a dentist, and want to avoid having to make an appointment on base, the best thing to do is to bring your most recent X-rays and request they be reviewed and your documents be signed instead of having an exam done. They may refuse, however, if they oblige, it will save you some time and headache. If you do have things that need to be corrected, like a large cavity, for example, they will most likely not sign it with the expectation you handle the issue with an outside provider, and then return with documentation saying it's been taken care of.

5. Once you've completed all portions of the screening, return to the office that issued it to you for final review to ensure there won't be any hiccups when you arrive.

6. Once you've been signed off on and reviewed, your service member will forward the necessary documents to their command so that their detailer can get the ball rolling on hard copy orders.

Pet Requirements

The process to import your pet to Japan is extensive, but straightforward. The steps and requirements are below:

1. Must be microchipped with a 16 digit microchip
2. Must have two rabies vaccines (be sure to have the two most recent ORIGINAL rabies certificates with you when you arrive in Japan)
3. FAVN blood test done 180 days prior to arrival - commonly referred to as "quarantine"
4. Advance notification 40 days prior to arrival sent to the airport of arrival (except if you are arriving in Yokota AFB via a military flight)
5. Health certificate issued within 10 days of ARRIVAL in Japan to be able to board the flight
6. Final paperwork inspection upon arrival
7. Pet physical and blood test with base veterinarian once you've arrived

The best thing you can do regarding your pet once you receive verbal orders to Japan is to schedule them for an appointment with a military veterinarian to make sure the first three things on that list are taken care of. The proper microchip, ensuring up to date vaccinations, specifically rabies, as well as starting their "quarantine" period by having their FAVN blood test done are critical pieces of the puzzle. If they need to update your pet's rabies vaccinations, be sure to keep their original certificate, as well as their previous one. You will be required to produce the two most recent rabies vaccination certificates upon arrival. If you can't, the 180-day quarantine clock resets, which can be very expensive if your pet needs to stay in a kennel during that time. I will discuss steps 4-7 more extensively in later chapters.

No Fee Passport

A no fee passport is different from a tourist passport. No fee passports are specifically for government-related travel, meaning you can only use it for flights when you are PCSing. Any other kind of travel requires a tourist passport. The Pentagon Foreign Clearance Guide is the authoritative document on entry requirements for service members and their families traveling on government orders around the world. This will tell you what kind of passport is required, if any, as well as any special visas, so please verify requirements based on your situation. The service member will be able to access the information from a navy computer. However, with that disclaimer out there, most families coming to Yokosuka are required to obtain a no fee passport for each accompanying dependent.

It is free and fairly easy to apply, just time consuming, which is why you can start the process with a letter of intent, and do not need to wait for hard copy orders or the family entry approval.

To start the application process, visit the passport office or PSD on your local base. They will be able to give you specific instructions or guidance on what you'll need to do. However, you may be able to take care of things in one trip if you have a current tourist passport, two passport photos, letter of intent, power of attorney, a DD form 1056, or branch equivalent, and a computer generated (*see note below) passport application. You may not need every single one of these components, as some offices vary in policies. However, I've generally found that if I don't have every single possible document that could potentially be necessary, I inevitably will have to make another trip back.

*The application form for a no fee passport is actually the same as a tourist passport. The paperwork is just routed differently, along with the Navy DD form 1056, or branch equivalent, which is a request for a no fee passport. To complete a passport application, you will simply need to go to the state department's website as if you were applying for a new passport, fill out an application, generate the printable PDF, and then print it, so you have a physical copy. While you're completing the form, if it asks you if you have had a passport before, PUT NO, since you're applying for a new no fee passport, not another tourist one. If you select yes, it will ask you a host of questions about what happened to your tourist one, which you want to avoid.

PCS Binder or Folder

This will be your best friend when you are moving. I suggest having one of these for every move, stateside or abroad. It is extremely helpful when you're in transit to have a centralized place to house all of your important documents. The military loves its paperwork, so if you're not organized, it's easy to lose things, or just feel like you're drowning in papers.

If you do a basic internet search for PCS binder, you'll find countless blog posts with tutorials on how to structure it, along with printable PDFs and all sorts of other resources. To be totally honest, I always found them to be overwhelming.

Many suggest a physical binder to put things into. I prefer to use a sturdy plastic accordion folder, and here's why. When you're checking in to a new command, you'll be running around between different offices, often with children in tow, or families waiting behind you. This makes time to neatly organize things into a 3-ring binder nearly nonexistent. You'll be expected to not only present documents but also receive them. It is much easier to keep things organized if you can simply throw papers into their appropriate folder pocket instead of having to break out a hole punch and open/close binder rings, to be able to put them away. Many suggest having a "catch all" folder in a binder that you can use to house all loose documents with the expectation of filing them later. However, I've found many people don't because, honestly, who has time for that? I highly recommend keeping things as simple as possible, especially when you're going to be navigating an already probably new and potentially stressful situation.

Here is a sample of how to organize your PCS folder, as well as which documents should be in it:

POA (powers of attorney)
- Be sure to have your service member go to your local legal office, or command equivalent, and get powers of attorney for anything you think you'll need to take care of in his or her stead. Generally, when you go, they will have a form that you can designate which special POAs you will need (i.e. ID cards, POVs, financial transactions, etc...). I recommend consulting with them about which ones they recommend for your move. However, many families end up ordering every special power of attorney on the menu, so that the dependent will be able to operate as if the service member isn't there in case they need to handle the checkout/ check in process solo.

PROPERTY
- Keep any documents pertaining to your pack out here such as inventory lists, pack out documentation, POV shipping/storage documents, furniture measurements, etc.

- House deeds, or vehicle titles. These will not necessarily be required for the check in process. However, they are difficult to replace if lost, so I highly recommend hand carrying them between duty stations versus sending them in your HHGs.

ORDERS

- Designate a folder specifically for orders, and have between 5-10 copies on hand. Many offices will want their own hard copy to have on file for the check in and check out process. A good tip to cut down on space is to skip the mostly blank first page and print the rest of the document double-sided. I also keep a set that is paper clipped instead of stapled in case an office says they're willing to make a copy, which helps mitigate the risk of running out.
- This tab is also where I kept my DEA, or dependent entry approval, and updated page 2 that you'll also need for checking in. Your service member will need to provide these to you.

HEALTH

- Have separate labeled folders for each dependent that have their overseas screening, as well as any medical, dental and immunization records that you'll need to have on hand. Medical records are not automatically transferred between duty stations, so I suggest trying to hand carry them if your current duty station will allow it.

- Pet Folders with Vaccination records, the 2 most recent ORIGINAL rabies vaccine certificates, original FAVN test results, health certificate for flights, any other documentation you have.

MISCELLANEOUS

- VALID driver's license. If your license is expired, renew it now as you will not be able to receive a SOFA driver's license without it.
- Tourist and no fee passports.
- Marriage License, birth certificates, social security cards. These will not necessarily be required for the check-in process. However, they are difficult to replace if lost, so I highly recommend hand carrying them between duty stations versus having them sent in your household goods shipment.
- Personal checks and emergency credit card(s) are great to have on hand in case of the unexpected.
- Notepad, Post its, Pens and paperclips are great to have on hand because you'll inevitably have to take notes, organize or label something at some point. Post its are fantastic because you'll be given several documents that need to be filled out and submitted to another office. For example, housing has forms that need to be completed and turned in to PSD or your service member's command so that you can qualify for different entitlements like OHA (overseas housing allowance), COLA (cost of living allowance)

or TLA (temporary lodging allowance). When receiving them, you can easily place a post-it note on each paper saying where it needs to go, and what supporting documents such as a hotel receipt, need to accompany it. This has been a sanity saver for me.

- Receipts will be required to get reimbursed for any covered out of pocket expenses, like hotels for example. I recommend an envelope to house them and ensure they don't go missing amidst the chaos.

- While it is necessary to have a physical binder to keep things in, I also keep a digital version of many critical documents, like orders and the Dependent Entry Approval for example, in an easily accessible folder on my phone. I do this so that when I write an email and need to attach something, I can do it without needing a computer. My preferred app for this is iCloud Drive, but others like Dropbox are also effective. For documents that you receive in paper format and want to convert to digital format, I recommend Camscanner. It's a free app that will automatically convert a picture of your document to an exportable PDF.

Budget

Moving overseas can be very expensive. Many out of pocket costs, like hotel accommodations, are eligible for reimbursement. However, others like buying a car, for example, are not. I always recommend to families that are PCSing, stateside and abroad, but particularly abroad, to take a look at their budget and make a plan for how they're going to deal with the expenses incurred during the move. The more time you have to save, the less stressful the financial piece of it will be.

Pack out Prep

Packing out is always a bit stressful. I often feel taken hostage by my belongings when it comes time to PCS. One of the best ways to combat this is to start preparing early. Figure out a system that works for you and allows you to purge and organize your home. I do not recommend trying to take it all on the week the movers arrive. This will most likely lead to unnecessary stress. One of my favorite things to do is to purge things that haven't been used in a while. Feel free to donate them, or even sell them. This is a great way to pad your PCS slush fund and mitigate many of those non reimbursable out of pocket costs. I will cover the nitty-gritty details of the actual pack out process, including tips for a smooth pack out and HHGs arrival day, in the coming chapters. These are best executed the week of your move though, so for now, focus on decluttering, organizing and purging.

3. HARD COPY ORDERS

When you receive hard copies of your orders, is when you can get into the meat and potatoes so to speak of your PCS. This is when you can schedule your pack out; make travel arrangements and book lodging, among other details that need to be finalized before making the jump to your new duty station. Here is a list of things in loose priority order that should be done.

1. Read the orders.
2. Schedule Travel
3. Schedule pack out
4. Arrange lodging
5. Arrange transportation
6. Get connected

Print and Read the Orders

This document will have valuable information like what date your service member needs to report by, contact information of your gaining command, things your service member may need to complete prior to arrival, and even entitlements. Think of this as the legend to your PCS roadmap.

Once you've read and understood the orders, save a digital version somewhere easily accessible and print several copies to place in your PCS folder. You will need extra copies to get the ball rolling on things like travel, household goods and, in some cases, lodging.

Schedule Travel

Travel arrangements are a key factor in your PCS, which is why I recommend you handle this as soon as you've received and read your orders. It is even more crucial to work these details out early if you plan on traveling with pets via a military flight, as there are only a certain number of pet spots available.

Commands handle travel arrangements differently, however, a good starting point if your current command isn't handling this part for you, is the travel office, or SATO. Think of them as the military version of a travel agency. If you need to travel on the government's dime, they are generally the ones who handle the tickets. For them to be able to book your tickets, they'll need a copy of orders, an applicable power of attorney if your service member isn't present, and your no fee passport, or proof that you've already applied for it if you haven't received it yet.

If you're traveling with a pet or pets, be aware that you are not allowed to bring more than two animals with you, and exotic pets are not allowed. If you have specific questions, I recommend reaching out to the housing office and/or base veterinarian clinic in Yokosuka for clarification.

Schedule Pack out

First thing to do when you're scheduling a pack out, is to go to your personal property office with orders, dependent/ family Entry Approval, or DEA, and a power of attorney if your service member won't be present. They'll be able to counsel you on when the best dates are based on how long it will take your things to arrive, what your entitlements are, such as what shipments you're allowed to have, as well as TLA or temporary lodging allowance. There are four different kinds of shipments that you'll most likely discuss. They are as follows:

1. **Express Shipment or Unaccompanied Baggage** - This is a smaller shipment that usually gets sent via air mail so that it arrives faster than your HHG shipment. This is supposed to be for sheets, blankets, pillows, towels, kitchen essentials, or anything else you'd like to arrive to hold you over until your regular shipment makes it to you, as it can take several months depending on where you are coming from. Housing has a furniture loaner program that you'll be able to take advantage of, so no furniture should be placed in this shipment. I have a list of helpful

items to include in this shipment in the reference section. Fleet and family also has loaner kitchen items. However, they are subject to availability, and it's generally easier and more comforting to have your own things. Please note, that even though it is sent via airmail, it still may take one to two months to arrive, so please plan accordingly, and have your shipment sent well ahead of time.

2. **HHG or Household Goods** - This is your main shipment and will include the rest of your belongings that you'd like sent.

3. **NTS or Non Temporary Storage** - If you're entitled to put things into storage, this would be something to take advantage of if you have large furniture that you're concerned won't fit into Japanese or base housing; items that will put your over your designated weight limit; or anything you'd rather not bring with you.

4. **POV or Personally Operated Vehicle** - People usually put their cars in storage because the costs associated with bringing an American car with you, and paying to have all of the modifications made for it to be road legal in Japan are extremely high. Buying a car once you arrive, is fairly simple and not too expensive in most cases. You can also easily get around town or the base on foot, by bicycle, or taxi. Be sure when putting your vehicle into storage that it is appropriately prepared by, at a minimum, arranging to have the battery disconnected and using fuel

stabilizer. Be sure to consult with the VPC, or vehicle processing center, as they will be able to give more in-depth guidance on this.

Once you've been counseled on what your entitlements are, you or your service member will have to create your shipments in DPS. DPS is the website used to create, coordinate and schedule military moves. When creating your DPS paperwork, be sure to include any special instructions for your shipment. Once you've done this, it will generate paperwork that will have to be printed and turned back into personal property either electronically or physically so that it can be processed. Once your shipments have been approved, you'll need to work with your designated moving company to finalize dates and any other details. They will generally come and do a survey at your home to determine the type and quantity of supplies they'll need. This includes specialty boxes for bulky items, such as televisions for example, or cranes/special equipment that may be necessary to hoist furniture out of a home if removing it via a balcony or window is the only option. If you have things like this, you should not only tell your counselor at personal property, but also put it into the notes of your DPS shipment application so that the appropriate moving company can be assigned to your pack out.

I also wanted to share some helpful hints about what to bring with you, and what to leave in storage. Yokosuka's base housing policy is currently involuntary MAH, or military assigned housing. This means that if the base has housing available that can accommodate you and your family; you have the options of either accepting it or living out in town at your own expense, which can be very pricey. The options given to you are based on what is available the day that you check into housing. The concept of moving somewhere and not having any idea of what kind of house you'll be living in, is enough to make anyone crazy, so I highly recommend you reach out to the housing office ahead of time and at the very least ask what kind of housing you're entitled to, based on your service member's rate/rank and family composition. Once you've found this out, take a look at the sample floor plans on CFAY's website, Pinterest or watch the video tours of some of the homes available on YouTube. This will give you a better idea of what you'll be able to fit into a home, what storage options there are, etc.

One of the best pieces of advice that I received was to measure all of my furniture before I packed out. This made it much easier when trying to select a house, and get settled because I knew for sure where pieces would fit where before our HHGs arrived. Our move in day went much smoother because I was able to have the movers place furniture where it would be going, instead of just having them drop it wherever so I could figure out the layout once they were done.

If you end up living out in town, the options have many more variables in terms of space or square footage, making the measurements even more critical.

Arrange Lodging

Now that you've been counseled by personal property on what your TLA entitlements are, and have approximate dates for your pack out and arrival in Japan, start making hotel arrangements. This includes while you are stateside between when your pack out happens, and when your flight leaves, as well as when you arrive in Japan. It may seem counterproductive to do this before you have exact dates nailed down; however, it is easier to slide things to the right or left by a day or two, than to try to book a 7-30 day window of time on short notice. If dates change, just call and amend your reservation. If you have pets, this is even more crucial to do as early as possible. Be sure to let them know you'll need a pet-friendly room, inquire about the associated costs so you can factor them into your budget, and be ready to produce current vaccination records at check-in, or beforehand via email.

Check with your personal property office to see how many days you are entitled to during each leg of your trip. As a rule of thumb, you should book your hotel room at the Navy Lodge in Japan for 30 days.

Arrange Transportation

As many people place their cars in storage, you should be able to handle this just days before your flight. Be sure to have arrangements to get around between when your drop your POV at the VPC, or Vehicle Processing Center, and when you're set to fly out. To make things easier, ensure that if you rent a vehicle, you can drop it directly at the airport the day of your departure.

Depending on if you arrive commercially, or on a military flight, commonly referred to as the rotator, getting to the base in Yokosuka will require using a Navy provided shuttle or the Japanese train system.

Arriving on a Military Flight

This is the military flight that leaves from SeaTac Airport in Seattle and flies directly to Yokota Air Force Base, which is located 36 miles from Yokosuka. That distance translates to a two to three-hour drive, possibly longer depending on traffic. When rotators arrive, they have a desk set up for people to sign up and utilize the shuttle to base. No Advanced reservation is necessary.

However, if you are arriving with a pet, you will not be allowed to utilize the shuttle and must make other arrangements. Best thing to do is to reach out to your receiving command (contact information should be on your orders) and see if they will make arrangements for you, ask your sponsor for help, or contact the Family Assistant and Support Team also known as the FAST office. There are also paid services available if all else fails.

Arriving at Narita

If you arrive in Narita, there is also a base shuttle available, or you can take the train. However, public transport could potentially be at your own expense. Check your orders, or with your receiving command's PSD to verify your entitlements. If you'd like to utilize the shuttle, you don't need to make an advanced reservation. However, it IS recommended to guarantee you a spot on the bus. Unfortunately, similar to the shuttle from Yokota, pets are not allowed, so you'll need to make alternate arrangements. Best thing to do is to reach out to your receiving command (contact information should be on your orders) and see if they will make arrangements for you, ask your sponsor for help, or contact the Family Assistant and Support Team, also known as the FAST office. There are also paid services available if all else fails.

Arrange Childcare

The waiting list for childcare can last up to a full year, so as soon as you receive orders and your Family Entry Approval documents, get your children on the list by going to the MWR website http://www.navymwryokosuka.com/child-youth and clicking the appropriate age option for your child. Once you do this, you'll see the link for the CEWL, or Central Enrollment Waiting List. Fill the form out and submit it. Be sure to follow up and ensure your form, and all necessary documents were received.

Get Connected

Knowledge is power, and while reading this book will help you with the majority of details concerning a move abroad, you will inevitably have more questions throughout the process. I highly recommend signing up for a spouse sponsor through the YESS program. This is a spouse who is in Yokosuka, specifically there to help you with your transition. They will be able to answer questions, or at least point you in the right direction for information and assist with things that may be tricky to handle while stateside.

A great first request is for them to add you to pertinent Facebook groups, so you can widen your net for information even more, and connect with other spouses before you arrive. There are groups for just about everyone!

Your spouse should be automatically assigned to a professional sponsor, but if you have little ones between the ages of 5 and 17, you can also sign them up for a sponsor through Fleet and Family! This could be a great way for your child to ease their anxiety, by being able to talk to someone who has been through what they're about to experience.

4. 30-60 DAYS BEFORE MOVING DAY

It is possible that you will receive orders within 30 to 60 days of your move date, but I thought it would be helpful, and less overwhelming, to separate the major tasks to tackle first from the nitty-gritty that can be done closer to your actual date of departure.

- Obtain FPO box (Can be issued up to 90 days before arrival) in Yokosuka & Forward mail
- Obtain medical, vaccination and dental records Make arrangements for pet's arrival
- Change Insurance policies Call Bank
- Children's school arrangements Cancel utilities
- Handle cell phone services
- Review employment and/or volunteer opportunities Get signed up for AOB
- Continue pack out preparations

Set Up FPO Box and Forward Mail

Your sponsor will be able to set up an FPO box for you up to 90 days out from your arrival date. Once they've been able to set this up, you'll be able to forward your mail, and even send things ahead of time that you may want to have when you arrive. Many retailers will ship to FPO/APO boxes, which is very convenient. The most common is Amazon. However, check shipping policies. Even if a retailer does ship to FPO/APO boxes, there are still weight/size limitations as well as restrictions on certain items, like bulky furniture or lithium batteries, for example. I usually like to forward my mail about a week or two before we are set to leave our current location to ensure we are able to collect anything that arrives after we have set up the forwarding service.

Obtain Medical, Vaccination and Dental Records

The easiest way to get registered at the hospital is to hand carry your documents from one installation to another. However, some bases will not allow dependents to do this, only service members. If this is the case, simply request that they be forwarded to your new base. The address they should be sent to is as follows:

OFFICIAL BUSINESS USNH YOKOSUKA
ATTN: MEDICAL RECORDS PSC 475 BOX 1 CODE 012A
FPO, AP 96350-9998

Make arrangements for your pet's arrival

Like I said in chapter two, the process to import your pet to Japan is extensive, but straightforward. The steps and requirements are below:

1. Must be microchipped with a 16 digit microchip
2. Must have two rabies vaccines (be sure to have the two most recent ORIGINAL rabies certificates with you when you arrive in Japan)
3. FAVN blood test 180 days prior to arrival - commonly referred to as "quarantine."
4. Advance notification 40 days prior to arrival
5. Health certificate issued within 10 days of ARRIVAL in Japan
6. Final paperwork
7. Import inspection upon arrival

At this point, you should have taken care of the first three things on the list above. What needs to happen now is you should schedule your pet's appointment for their health certificate within 10 days of your projected arrival date. I recommend having the appointment take place 5 days before, to allow a few days of wiggle room in case your flight gets delayed.

You'll also need to complete the paperwork on the Japanese website, maff.go.jp and submit it to the proper airport if you're flying commercially. If you're arriving on a military flight into Yokota air base, this isn't necessary.

You should also reach out to your gaining command to have them set a shuttle up for you and your family as you won't be able to take advantage of the usual shuttle. (See "Arrange

Transportation" section of Chapter 3: Hard Copy Orders, for more information on how to arrange a private shuttle)

Change Insurance Policies and Update Mailing Address

Call your current insurance provider and have them amend your policies based on your new situation, as well as update your mailing address to your new FPO box. Be sure to have them update your personal property/renter's insurance. If you don't have this, I highly recommend it. Also, be sure to either place your automobile insurance on a plan that covers it in storage or cancel it if you are selling your vehicle before your move.

Call Your Bank

Call your bank and credit card companies to let them know that you'll be traveling internationally. This will mitigate the risk of you having a card frozen, or transaction declined while you're in transit. While you have them on the phone, also update mailing addresses. This piece can usually also be done online. However, I tend to handle both at the same time in the spirit of efficiency.

Make Arrangements for Schooling

This would be the time to contact your children's current school, to obtain any necessary records for their future enrollment, and also reach out to the school they will be attending to get them enrolled.

For this you will need:

1. A copy of orders
2. Family Entry Approval,
3. Student's passport or a copy of their birth certificate
4. DOD immunization form. Other records will not be accepted. This is the website for what immunizations are required http://www.dodea.edu/parents/immunizations.cfm
5. Depending on the age of your child, a physical will also be required

Cancel Utilities, Subscriptions and Memberships

Be sure to cancel any recurring subscriptions or memberships as well as your utilities and make arrangements to return any equipment, like cable boxes or modems. Many companies require at least 30 days' notice, to avoid early cancellation or other unnecessary fees.

Handle Cell Phone Services Stateside

Check with your carrier what your options are in terms of 1. If you should cancel your service, 2. Continue with them if they offer an international plan that suits your needs, or

3. Place your plan on military suspension. (See the "get cell service" section of Chapter 7: The First Two Weeks, for more information about cell phone plans in Japan)

Review Employment Opportunities

If you're interested in working and/or volunteering while in Yokosuka, there are many opportunities on and off base to volunteer and work. Some great resources to check for on base employment are the Navy Exchange and MWR (Morale Welfare and Recreation). The Navy Exchange, or NEX, lists their jobs on the following website: www.mynavyexchange.com/nex/work-for-us.

Another great website to check for other opportunities is usajobs.gov.

Many spouses also choose to start a home business, work as an English teacher, or do modeling!

Get Signed Up for AOB

Your sponsor can take care of this for you, or you can send an email to FFSCINFO@fe.navy.mil with your full name(s), the name of your service member's gaining command, and the date you'd like to take the class. Be sure to put AOB/ICR in the subject line. If you have little ones, they will be able to provide you with the options for childcare during that week.

Continue Pack Out Prep and Send Express Shipment*

Depending on long it takes for your things to arrive in Japan, you may potentially want to send your express shipment, aka unaccompanied baggage, one to two months early. I usually will send the things that I like the most, ahead of time, instead of things we feel we can live without, like spare sheets that generally stay in the closet. Reason being is so that it feels easier exiting our old home, and more exciting and homey when we arrive and get settled in our new one.

See the Reference section for a helpful list of suggested items to send.

Here are some other helpful things to do in preparation of your impending pack out:

- Begin bagging hanging clothes in trash bags, and use the ties to keep hangers together and organized. Label each bag, so you can easily identify its contents, and know where it should be stored. For example: coats, uniforms, formal dresses, Jane's closet, John's closet, etc…
- Use Vacuum seal bags for linens, towels, or seasonal clothes that you won't use before your pack out date.

Throw a dryer sheet into the makeshift garment bags and vacuum seal bags so that the contents arrive smelling fresh as they will be in transit for quite a while.

5. WEEK OF THE MOVE

The week of your move will most likely be a little crazy regardless of how much prep work you do ahead of time. The best way to stay ahead of the crazy is to anticipate it and keep your daily workload manageable. Don't try to do everything in one day, especially if you have little ones. Try to break things up so that you don't feel like you're climbing a mountain, but more like a hill. This will be the difference of being in tears at the end of the day or having a glass of wine on the couch after you've completed your to-do list feeling accomplished and ready for whatever tomorrow holds.

Here is how I usually break down my week of a move.

Day One:
- Pack Suitcases. I love to use packing cubes for different things to keep my suitcases organized. I have a small one for socks and underwear, a larger one for pants and tops, and one for toiletries. This has been a lifesaver when going through airport security if I have to unpack and then repack my suitcase! It also helps if you want to pack things ahead of time. If you don't want to invest in packing cubes, use large zip-lock bags, these are even better if you plan on using

one suitcase for several children since you can label them!

- Forward mail if you haven't already. You can do this on the post office's website.

Day Two:

- Pull pictures off of the walls and tape hardware to the back with painter's tape to make hanging at your next home more convenient
- Place painter's tape on mirrors/glass pieces to help avoid cracking or damage in transit
- Place any remaining clothes/linens/towels into space saver bags, or trash bags with dryer sheets to ensure freshness upon arrival

Day Three:

- Separate out things going into the different shipments. Don't be afraid to separate things into different rooms, group things together, or use color-coded post-it notes to make things easy on the movers. The simpler the system, the less room for error!
- Use large ziplock bags to group kitchen drawer contents together, to help ease unpacking in your new home. Be sure not to bag anything going into Express Shipment if it hasn't already been sent!

Day Four:

- Print labels with your name and email for boxes. This is more of a "nice to have," than a necessity. In theory, your movers should crate your boxes in your presence to ensure everything arrives safely and intact. However, this isn't always the case. Things happen. The best way for someone to get your things back to you is if your information is clearly marked on the boxes. A simple label with your name and email will save you a lot of time and heartache if something goes missing! The easiest way to make this happen is to print some peel and stick labels for the boxes. Don't be afraid to print more than you need, as you'll be able to use them for your next move as well!

- Prepare any necessary inventories. This is if you have a wine collection, firearms, or high-value items. Your personal property office or moving company should be able to provide more in-depth guidance on this.

- Prepare your moving legend. This will be helpful the day you receive your household goods. Many have found that using different colored duct tape to label boxes that go into certain rooms, and then placing a legend for mover's to see so they know exactly where things need to go to be very helpful. For example, red duct tape for the master bedroom, blue for the kitchen, etc. The movers should label the boxes, but for a mover, knowing what colored box goes into different rooms is easy and intuitive. It saves them having to ask you where each box should go and saves you the headache of moving things around if they get put in the wrong spot. Be sure to keep the legend as well as some extra of each tape on sheets of paper in your PCS bible to be able to utilize the day you receive your things in your new home. You'll be able to not only post the legend but also tape the extra scraps of tape to the doors of the room where they go.

Day Five:
- Pre-make some freezer meals if you don't want to eat out! This is nice to do if you don't want to eat fast food once your things have all been packed up. PCSing is typically tough on your waistline, as well as your wallet, so this is a great way to save both!
- Veterinarian appointment for health certificate to fly. This needs to be done within ten days of arrival. It's best to have a few days of wiggle room in case your flights are delayed.
- Prepare your kennel with any necessary supplies your pet may need such as food, water, leash, treats and something comfortable to line the bottom of their kennel while they're in transit.

Day Six:
- Return utility equipment like cable box or modem.
- Do laundry. Throw any remaining clothes in the wash so that you don't have dirty laundry coming to greet you in your new home!

Moving Day:

- Run the dishwasher first thing in the morning, so you don't have any dirty dishes getting packed up in your household goods
- Wash the sheets, towels, and bathmats that are getting packed in your express shipment. If your movers are arriving very early, tell them to pack your express shipment last so that your sheets, towels and bath mats have time to finish washing and drying before they are packed to avoid any mildewing.**
- Take the trash out and wipe the trash can down so that it goes into your express shipment nice and clean!**

** If you express shipment is getting packed up the same day as your HHG shipment.

6. ARRIVING

Surviving a long haul flight isn't easy for anyone, especially if you have children. Traveling solo can be stressful enough, but when you're moving your life and family across the world, it's a whole other level of crazy and stressful. To help keep the stress at a minimum, do your best to travel as light as possible, give yourself LOTS of time at the airport, so you're not rushing around, and try to stay flexible. If you have a good attitude, then the inevitable hiccups that occur won't throw you into a downward spiral. No one wants that! I've listed some tips below to help you and your family survive a long haul flight, and also outlined how to get to base once you've landed in Japan.

Tips on how to survive a long-haul flight

- Bring entertainment. Load an iPad up with your favorite series, or bring a favorite book...the flight will most likely have some things to help keep you entertained, but there's no guarantee they will have something you're interested in. This also includes some comfortable headphones. They'll most likely provide some inflight, but they don't produce the best sound quality and usually end up hurting my ears.

- Dress accordingly. Flights tend to be either very warm or icy cold. Dress in comfortable, breathable layers so that you'll be able to accommodate either. My go-to outfit consists of stretchy cotton pants, a comfortable t-shirt layered with a cardigan and long scarf. I also bring warm, comfortable socks, and shoes that slip on and off easily.

- Pack some toiletry essentials. You will sleep better if you go through your nightly routine. I personally brought face wash and lotion, a toothbrush and toothpaste for when I was trying to fall asleep, as well as my makeup bag, dry shampoo, comb, some baby wipes and a fresh set of clothes for when I wanted to freshen up about an hour before the plane landed.

- Drink lots of water. I have a favorite leak-proof bottle that I like to bring with me so that I can fill it up throughout the journey to stay hydrated without breaking the bank. Sometimes, the flight attendants are nice enough to fill it for me when they do their drink service instead of giving me a cup.

- Have some healthy TSA approved snacks. They will feed you on the flight, but airplane food isn't the best. I like to have some low sodium options like peanut butter crackers, cut veggies, or almonds.

- Don't be afraid to use sleep aids. My personal favorite is melatonin or lavender oil. Melatonin for flights is a safer bet as people around you may be sensitive to smells. However, once I've checked with those around me, I like being able to put it on my feet and neck. It's very a very soothing natural alternative. If those don't seem to excite you, then there are plenty of other over the counter options available like ZZZquill, or Unisom.

- Have a mini emergency kit. I like to carry hand sanitizer, wipes, tissues, basic medications (ibuprofen, anti-diarrheal, tums and melatonin), a tampon/panty liner, Band-Aids, rewetting eye drops/ Visine, tube of Vaseline, Emergen-C, extra set of contacts, Shout wipe, Safety pins/sewing kit, extra hair ties and bobby pins, cash, along with some other things. This may sound like overkill, but I generally tend to use the majority of these things and actually carry this with me daily since they fit in a small change purse that's slightly larger than the dimensions of a credit card, with the exception of the wipes, hand sanitizer and tissues. It's gotten me out of countless sticky situations, so I tend to never leave home without it! As for my preflight ritual, I like to take Emergen-C an hour before I board the flight to help make sure I don't catch anything from a fellow traveler, use some antibacterial wipes to clean the area around me once I've gotten into my seat, and use the Vaseline to keep my lips hydrated, and have even used it to coat the inside of my nose if it's feeling dry or irritated.

- If you wear contacts, I highly recommend bringing your glasses, and a contacts case pre-filled with solution, a small mirror and some rewetting drops. Flights are always super dry, so this will allow you to either rewet your eyes or take your contacts out if necessary and still be able to see. I like to keep all these together in my glasses case, so they're easy to access.

- Have a cords/electronics bag. I use a small nylon zipper bag to keep all charging cords, external battery packs and electronics in. It makes it easy to find them, and also keeps me from fighting them when trying to find other things! If you don't want to buy a bag, a ziplock will work just fine as well.

Tips on how to survive a long haul flight with kids

- Dress for the schedule you want them to get on.
- If you want them to sleep on the flight, dress them in, or bring their pajamas. To help them wake back up once you've landed, don't be afraid to execute your morning routine in the airport restroom. Get them changed, brush their teeth, comb their hair. You'll have plenty of time to do this as bags take a bit to come through at baggage claim.
- Get a tot cot or Jet-Kid suitcase. These are basically gadgets made to fill the space between the edge of the seat and the back of the one in front of them, making a larger surface for your little one to sleep on. Not only will they be more comfortable, but you will be too not having a child on your lap!

- Bring lots of entertainment for them. iPads with their favorite shows downloaded, external battery packs and charging cords to ensure the iPad or your phone doesn't die, window clings if you happen to get a window seat, coloring books, snacks (note: Most fresh fruits will be confiscated by customs upon arrival)...you know your child best, so pack whatever you know will keep them entertained.
- Have a mini emergency kit. I like to carry hand sanitizer, wipes, tissues, basic medications (pain reliever, anti-diarrheal, antacid and melatonin), a tampon/panty liner, Band-Aids, eye drops, tube of Vaseline, Emergen-C, extra set of contacts, Shout wipe, Safety pins/sewing kit, extra hair ties and bobby pins, cash, along with some other things.

How to prep your animal's kennel

Be sure to double check the regulations of whatever operator or carrier you're flying. However, the rule of thumb for carrier size is that your pet must be able to stand up and turn around comfortably. They will also need a day's worth of food and water either in the kennel in an approved container, or taped to the outside. I've seen this done a multitude of ways. Some families will tape a ziplock bag full of food to the top and zip tie a small water bottle to the front of the kennel if they do not want their pet to have access to it during the flight but will want to feed them once they've arrived.

Some carriers require you to have food bowls fastened to the front of the kennel. You can either purchase bowls specifically for this purpose or poke holes in small ziplock/Gladware containers and use zip ties to secure them. To ensure water isn't sloshing around and getting your pet or their carrier wet while they're being put on the plane, I recommend freezing water in a bowl, or using some ice cubes.

You also will NOT be turned away if your kennel is bigger than your pet needs. Generally, the pet and kennel just need to be under 50 pounds (again, check regulations of whatever carrier you're flying). When we flew with our cat, we had a large dog kennel, and lined the bottom of the carrier with bags of essentials we knew we would need upon arrival including two large ziplock bags of kitty litter, a small ziplock of litter box liners, a large ziplock bag of extra food, a bag of treats, a bag with the extra nuts bolts for the carrier, a bag with a harness and leash, as well as bags of extra house training pads, some grocery bags to help with clean up, travel package of Clorox wipes and his soft sided carrier collapsed so it laid flat. I arranged it all as even and flat as possible and then laid a comfortable, cushy blanket over top of everything. I put a small box with a house training pad in it as well as a litter scoop, at the back of the kennel in case he needed to relieve himself, as well as a small cat bed in the front with his travel food and water bowls next to him in case he was hungry. We love the pet food travel system from Kurgo because they're soft-sided and can fold down very small, but are large enough for daily use while in transit. This eased our anxiety knowing that he was arguably more comfortable on the flight than we were. However, it was also self-serving because we knew upon arrival we had everything we needed for him without having to run to a store, or carry an extra piece of luggage stocked with pet supplies. As the pet kennel was rather large and bulky, we generally would travel with it broken down since the top half folded into the bottom one, and carry him in his soft-sided carrier. Folding the two halves into each other kept everything in place, and we were able to put our carryon luggage or a sea bag inside to save space.

While this strategy may be difficult to execute with a larger dog, it is possible to utilize the extra space for things you may want to have once you've arrived like a leash, harness, plastic bags for clean up, extra food (I recommend storing this outside of the kennel), travel food bowls, or toys. I also like to travel with a travel size pack of Clorox wipes and an extra grocery/trash bag in the event of an accident. No one, pet or human, wants to ride in a car containing a dirty kennel.

How to get to base from the airport

Military flight into Yokota (aka rotator)
If you arrive via the rotator, or military flight to Yokota, you will deplane and have a customs brief before you can collect your luggage and pets. Once you've done this, you will have

two options of arriving on base. The first is the base provided shuttle. No advanced sign up is required, you will simply go and visit the representative and sign in for it. If you are arriving with pets, you will need to make alternative arrangements since animals are not allowed in the shuttle buses. More information on this is provided in the "make travel arrangements" section of Chapter 3: Hard Copy orders.

Commercial flight into Narita WITHOUT pets

When you arrive at Narita, you'll deplane and be expected to go through customs and immigration. They will need to stamp your no-fee passport with two stamps. The first will be the regular stamp that would be placed into anyone's passport coming into the country. The second is a sofa stamp that should have the following:

Under Status of Forces Agreement
Entered Japan:
Date:
Port:
Immigration Inspection:

For this to happen, the immigration officer will need your passport and/or ID card, a hard copy of your orders and completed immigration paperwork that was provided on the plane. As a courtesy to others in line, please complete the form before you get to the window.

Once you've cleared immigration, you'll proceed with your stamped paperwork, collect your baggage and then proceed to customs. You'll need to go to the long counter marked "non-resident." After you've done this, you can finally start your journey to the base.

If you're taking public transportation, it could possibly be at your own expense. Check with your gaining command on what your entitlements are. The easiest route is to use the base provided shuttle. If you'd like to utilize the shuttle, you don't need to make an advanced reservation. However, it *is* recommended to guarantee you a spot. You can do this by calling 011-81-46-816-777 ahead of time. I recommend using the Skype app to call, so you avoid any pricey long distance fees.

To find the shuttle, exit into the arrivals lobby of Terminal one and head to the North wing, where you'll find the transportation desk directly across from the farthest left exit. If you arrive in terminal two, there's a free shuttle that will take you to Terminal one from bus stops 8 or 18. If you exit into the south wing, ask someone for directions. Japanese customer service is amazing, and they will most likely take you there personally.

The desk can be identified by a small sign. This is purposeful, to protect service members and their families and promote OPSEC/PERSEC. It may say in your orders, that the desk is located at the Northwest Airlines information counter. However, it is not. When you arrive, there should be a representative there. If there's not, they may be showing a group of people to the buses and will eventually return. There will be a sign explaining departure times, as well as a courtesy phone that you can use to call your command or sponsor.

Commercial flight into Narita WITH pets

When you arrive at Narita, you'll deplane and be expected to go through customs and immigration. They will need to stamp your no-fee passport with two stamps. The first will be the regular stamp that would be placed into anyone's passport coming into the country; the second is a sofa stamp that should have the following:

Under Status of Forces Agreement
Entered Japan:
Date:
Port:
Immigration Inspection:

For this to happen, the immigration officer will need your passport and/or ID card, a hard copy of your orders and completed immigration paperwork that was provided on the plane. As a courtesy to others in line, please complete the form before you get to the window.

Once you've cleared customs, you'll be able to collect your pet and baggage in the baggage claim area. Once you get your pet, you'll need to have your paperwork inspected at the medical/quarantine desk. Be sure to keep all your documentation for your pet together and start your journey to the base.

Unfortunately, similar to the shuttle from Yokota, pets are not allowed, so you'll need to make alternate arrangements ahead of time. If this is the case, best thing to do is to reach out to your receiving command (contact information should be on your orders) and see if they will make arrangements for you, ask your sponsor for help, or contact the FAST (Family Assistant and Support Team- contact info available in appendix). There are also paid services available if all else fails. Information to have ready when making arrangements includes number of people, pets, luggage and dimensions of the kennel you'll be using.

Ways to get around base once you've arrived

Bus - There is a bus that runs through base. When you check into the Lodge, they will most likely give you a schedule of when and where they run to. If they do not, simply request one. It is free to use, however, runs intermittently and is fairly slow going as it makes many stops.

Walk - Most places on base are accessible on foot. From one side of base to the other, it's approximately 2 miles.

Taxi - Taxis are also an easy way to get around. They have on base taxis that you can call from your hotel room, or the courtesy phone in the lobby of the lodge, located by the entrance. They will run you between $5 and $7. They accept yen and dollars. There are also off base taxis. However, they will take a bit longer to arrive since they are subject to an extra security measure upon entering the base. Phone numbers are in the appendix.

Bicycles - Bikes are a great way to get around base, or out into town. If you want to get a bike, I recommend either checking out the NEX at the Fleet Rec Center or going out in town. Generally, the bicycles out in town will be a bit cheaper and have more required features included, like a front and back light, bike lock and bell. If you do buy a bike, you will need to register it with base security before you can take it off base. You are also required to wear a helmet while riding it. If you buy a bike out in town, my recommendation is the store Livin. They have a great selection of bicycles that aren't too expensive and have almost all the required bells and whistles. They will also, for a small fee of about $5, register your bike with the city of Yokosuka, so you don't have to make an extra trip to do so, to be able to ride/park it out in town.

Where to eat

Once you've arrived at the Lodge, Chili's is the closest

restaurant and is about a two to three-minute walk from the hotel. There are also some delivery options available on base depending on what time of day it is. Check the appendix for a list of places to eat on base as well as their locations, and contact information.

Where to get cash

There are multiple ATMs located around the base. There is a list of them and which kinds of currency they dispense located in the Appendix.

7. THE FIRST TWO WEEKS

- Cell phone
- Check into command Housing
- Post Office Personal Property
- Hospital outpatient records, Tricare, dental Personnel Support Detachment (PSD) Security
- School/Childcare* Veterinarian* Utilities
- CFAY legal*
- Vehicle Registration Office (VRO) AOB
- Locations, hours of operation and contact numbers are listed below for each location

*If applicable

Cell phone

Pretty much anything you do on base will require an address and cell phone number for contact information. To avoid having to double back, I recommend getting your cell phone squared away before checking in anywhere. Here are the options on and off base. But before you go anywhere or make decisions, if you're considering using your smartphone, you need to check the regulatory settings to make sure it will work in Japan. To do this on an iPhone, go to settings >

General > Regulatory. Once you click on this, you'll be able to see what countries your phone will work in. If you don't see Japan, then your phone will not work, even if it's "unlocked." Android products vary. There are resources available online, or I would reach out to your carrier for specific instructions for your model. Next, you need to make sure it's "unlocked," meaning you can put any SIM card in regardless of carrier and it will work. If it's not, you can do this with the carrier you purchased it from.

Another tip is that regardless of the company you decide to go with for service, be sure to set up service in whoever's name will be doing maintenance on it. If your name is not on the account, they will not allow you to do anything without a power of attorney. Even with a POA, they will still give you a hard time. An easy way around this is to put both lines in whoever's name, usually, the spouse if the service member will be deploying, will be doing any of the upkeep like changing plans or paying the bill.

Softbank - they are available on base and will allow you to use your phone. Smartphone plans range around $80/ month per line for a two-year contract. There is also an approximate $200 cancellation fee PER LINE if you need to cancel before or after your contract is up. A less expensive option is a $15/month plan for a flip phone that you can only use to make calls.

AU - They are just outside of the gate and have similar prices to Softbank, however, will not allow you to use your own device. Policies are always changing though, so be sure to check with them if you're dead set on using your own phone.

Project Fi - Google recently started Project Fi. It's basically a phone service that piggybacks off of various carrier networks pretty much anywhere in the world and starts at $20/month for one line, and $15/month to add up to 5 additional lines with no monthly contract. If you go over your data allotment, there's no penalty; you're simply charged $10/GB. The catch is that you must use a Google Pixel or certain Nexus phones. They range between $249 to around $900 and it must be set up while physically in the United States.

Other Simcards - There are companies that offer data-only SIM cards that you may see online, but many require a Japanese credit card for activation which can be difficult to obtain.

Check into command

In order to stop your leave and start your entitlements like TLA, your service member will have to check into their command. The information on how to do this, like who to contact and where to go, will be written in their orders.

Housing

Once you've checked into your command, you'll need to go to the housing brief with a copy of your orders, Family Entry Approval, Updated Page 2, and any other necessary supporting documents. Some examples are pet documentation, legal custody agreement or page 2 for dependents with a different last name, proof of pregnancy, power of attorney if you'll be attending in your service member's stead, flight itinerary for dependents on delayed travel, promotion letter if rank will be different from what is listed on your orders, PRD extension letter if your PRD is different from your orders, etc. Briefs are held in the housing office, which is the same building as the Navy Lodge, at 8:15 AM (check in is at 8 AM) Monday through Friday except for holidays and the first Wednesday of every month. This is where the service member is given all of the information concerning what housing options you have. They'll be given a list of options based on rank, family composition and what is available that day. Most families are required to live on base unless there is not something that can accommodate their family or pet. If this is the case, they will put you in touch with reputable real estate agents who will take you to tour homes off base. If you only qualify for on base housing, they'll give you the list of what's available to you and depending on the unit; you'll be able to tour it, or something comparable. This will feel like a high-pressure sales situation. Just remember, you don't have to sign for anything the moment you receive the list. There are potentially other families that are in competition for the same unit, so it's to your benefit to weigh going to see the house or signing for it immediately. But know you have options. Reviewing the video tours on YouTube, and floor plans available online will help ease some of the anxiety of signing for something sight unseen.

Before leaving the brief, they'll give you a time to come back and meet with your housing counselor to sign for your new home on base. Once you do, they'll go through some other paperwork with you. First, they'll have you choose the loaner furniture you'd like to have until your things arrive and schedule the delivery for you. They'll also give you a TLA document to fill out and submit to your command, so you get reimbursed for your hotel. Next, will be a parking spot document. If you buy a car, you'll need this to register it at the VRO, or Vehicle Registration Office, on base. They'll also give you a document to submit to PSD so that your entitlements, like COLA and OHA, can start. I highly recommend having post-it notes on hand to label each sheet of paper with what it is, where it needs to go, and what supporting documents, like receipts, for example, should accompany it.

Post Office

Most offices will want a phone number and address when checking in. Your sponsor can set up a post office box for you up to 90 days out from your arrival date with a set of orders and your Family Entry Approval. This is great so that you can forward your mail and have a seamless transition from one home to another. If you don't have this done ahead of time, the process is simple once you arrive. You'll just need to go to the post office and find the window between the area where you send packages, and pick them up between 8 and 4 Tuesday through Thursday, with your military ID, copy of orders, the family entry approval and power of attorney if your service member won't be there. There's a short form to fill out, and they issue you a box on the spot. The only reason that some people wait until they arrive and receive housing is in case they end up living in Ikego as they have a post office there as well. Some people don't want to make the journey to the main base, just to check their mail.

Personal Property

Now that you've been assigned housing, if you've received the email that your things have arrived, you can call personal property to schedule the delivery of your express shipment and household goods. Housing does not do this for you. The contact information is located in the appendix.

Hospital

Next, head to the hospital. You'll check in with medical records and TRICARE which are located to the left when you walk in the main entrance. Once you've done this, head upstairs and check in with dental. If you have your medical and dental records, bring them with you so that they do not have to make you a new physical folder. This makes the check-in process a bit smoother. If you were unable to hand carry them, ask them for a <u>medical record request form</u> and <u>send it to your previous duty station</u>.

Transfer of medical records is not automatic and must be <u>prompted by the service member or their family</u>.

Security

You'll need to <u>check in at security or go to the FAST</u> office located in the same building as AOB, where they'll add your <u>ID card</u> to their central database called DBIDs. This isn't necessary to get on and off base, but it is necessary if you plan on buying a car since you'll need to register it with security.

PSD

This is where you'll hand in your updated page 2 as well as the paperwork you received from housing concerning your entitlements.

School/Childcare

Stop by, or make an appointment at the facilities necessary to drop any paperwork necessary to get your children enrolled in their respective schools or care facilities.

Veterinarian

If you have pets, you must go to the Veterinarian's office located behind the fire station to turn in your paperwork, register your pet on base, and make an appointment for your final quarantine exam. The pet does not need to be with you for this step, only for the final quarantine exam. When you set up the appointment, you'll be required to surrender your pet's documents for review, and they will be given back to you when you have your final exam.

Utilities

Once you receive your housing assignment, you'll need to set up your utilities. If you live on base, your electric and water are automatically taken care of, but you'll need to set up your internet and phone service.

Internet on base is provided through Americable. To set up services, you'll need to go to their office with your housing assignment paperwork, a POA if your service member won't be present (regardless of whether or not they will be present, I recommend putting it in your name if you'll be doing the maintenance on the account like bill pay, or changing plans), and the credit or debit card you'll be using for automatic payments. Service starts the same day, and they will give you your equipment on the spot, including cables, so you can simply plug everything in when you get home and start utilizing it. Americable is also a VPN blocker, so you'll be able to use American streaming services like Netflix, HULU and Pandora for example if you're connected to their internet.

Getting a DSN line for your home on base is free. You'll just need to go to the BCO (Base Communications Office) located in the PSD Building with a copy of your orders, Family Entry Approval, housing documentation and a power of attorney if you service member won't be there. Having a DSN is convenient not only for calling numbers on base but also because you can call American toll free numbers. Be sure to also request a base directory. It's a very useful book that has a comprehensive list DSN numbers on base.

CFAY Legal

If you plan on starting a home business, head to CFAY legal on command hill to pick up your home business application. Once you've completed it, you'll need to submit it to your service member's command for endorsement. Once you have command endorsement, hand it in at the housing facilities office located on the ground floor of Bara heights, which is across the street from the regular housing office (next to the Navy Lodge). Once you do that, your paperwork will be routed through housing, then the NEX and then base JAG for approval. If approved, you'll receive an official letter stating that you are CFAY approved to do business on base.

VRO (Vehicle Registration Office)

If you plan on buying a car, there are several resources available to you. Many families resell their vehicles when they PCS, or there are several dealerships whose niche is American families. There is also a "lemon lot" by the Commissary that has a mix of vehicles up for sale by families, and dealerships. If you buy from a dealership, chances are they will handle all of the paperwork for you. If you buy from someone in a private sale, you'll most likely have to deal with the paperwork which is extensive, but fairly straightforward. To get the ball rolling, you'll need to purchase insurance. There are two companies, both associated with USAA, which are available to buy from in the VRO office. Once you have insurance, you will head to the Vehicle Registration Office for them to transfer the car into your name. This is not a title transfer, just so the base knows who the vehicle belongs to. Once that has happened, they will provide you with the necessary paperwork for you to schedule your car inspection at the autoport on base which is just around the corner from the VRO behind the NEX minimart. Once you've completed your inspection, you'll need to register your vehicle with the government of Japan. There are several home businesses that we handle this for you for a fee of around $50. They essentially take your paperwork to the Japanese VRO equivalent in Yokohama to purchase your JCI and transfer the title into your name. I recommend visiting the VRO and picking up a packet of information on how to purchase and register a vehicle based on your situation as they will have the most up to date policies and procedures on hand.

Another common option for getting around is buying a bike. You can either purchase one from the Fleet Rec NEX, or there are several stores out in town, like Livin' that sell them. Once you purchase a bicycle, you'll need to register it with base security. They will need the bike physically there to inspect. You'll need proof of purchase, or your HHG paperwork showing it came with you from your previous duty station, and all the required safety features (helmet, bell, front and back lights, lock, etc...)

AOB

Once you've arrived, service members and their spouses (as well as dependents in some cases depending on their age) are required to attend AOB, or area orientation brief. It is a 4 day class that teaches you about base policies, amenities as well as Japanese culture. You will need to sign up in advance. (See "Get Signed Up For AOB" section in Chapter 4: 30-60 Days Before Moving Day).

Useful Information for Checking In

Cell phone
SOFTBANK
Building 1559 (Next to Starbucks across from the NEX)
Phone: 046-896-2001
Hours: Open daily from 10:00-20:00

AU

2 Chrone - 2 3 Ōdakichō Yokosuka-shi, Kanazawa-Ken 238-0008

Phone: 0800-700-0962

Hours: Open daily from 10:00-20:00

Check into command

Contact information for your command will be listed in your orders.

Housing

Building 1441 (Entrance is to the right of the Navy Lodge Entrance)

Phone: DSN 243-9037

Regular 046-816-9037

Hours: Monday-Friday 08:00-16:30

Except for the first Wednesday of the month 11:00-16:30

Post Office

Building 1258

Phone: DSN 243-5486

Regular 046-816-5486

Hours: Post Office

Tuesday through Saturday 0900-1600

Sundays and Holidays Closed

Parcel Pick up

Monday through Saturday 0900-1600

Sundays and Holidays Closed

Personal Property
Building 5013
Phone: DSN 243-7587
Regular 046-816-7587
Hours: Monday through Friday 0800-1600
Except Wednesday 0800-1500

Hospital
Outpatient records, Tricare, dental Building 1400
Phone: DSN 243-5247 or 243-7144
Regular 046-816-5247 or 046-816-7144
Hours: Monday through Friday 730-1630
General Care Emergency Room 24/7

PSD (Personnel Support Detachment)
Building 1555
Phone: DSN 243-6813 or 243-8457
Regular 046-816-7587
Hours: Monday 0900-1600 Tuesday 0730-1630
Wednesday 0900-1500 Thursday 0730-1630
Friday 0900-1600 Saturday & Sunday Closed

AOB (Area Orientation Brief)
Building G45 (Across from the Commissary) or Benny
Decker Theatre

Security
Located at Main Gate
Phone: DSN 243-2300 or 243-2301
Regular 046-816-2300 or 046-816-2301
For Emergencies, dial 911 from a DSN, or 046-816-0911 for on base Security.
Hours: 24/7

Veterinarian
Building H1230 (behind the CFAY Fire Station)
Phone: DSN 243-6820
Regular 046-816-6820
Hours: Monday-Wednesday and Friday 9:00-15:30
Closed Thursday, Saturday and Sunday as well as the last Friday of every month and holidays

CFAY legal
Building 1472 (next to Human Resources Office on Command Hill)
Phone: DSN 243-7335
Regular 046-816-7335
Hours: Monday-Friday 7:30-16:30
Closed Saturday & Sunday

Vehicle Registration Office (VRO)
Building J196
Phone: DSN 243-5011
Regular 046-816-5011

Hours: Monday-Friday 0830-1530

Closed Saturday & Sunday and all US Holidays

Utilities

Americable

Building B-39 (behind CPO club)

Phone: DSN 241-2288

DSN Setup

Base Communications Office (BCO)

2nd Floor of Building 1555 (PSD Building)

Phone: DSN 243-4600

Regular 046-816-4600

8. REFERENCE

Navy Exchange Store Locations & Services

Main store
Apparel & Shoes, Handbags, Jewelry & Accessories, Cosmetics & Fragrances, Health & Beauty, Household Goods, Books & Magazines, Stationery, Toys, Snacks & Beverages, Consumer electronics (Apple, Bose & Sony Shops), Gaming & Entertainment.

Flower Shop
Balloons, Gift Items & Flowers, Delivery on Yokosuka and Ikego Bases.

Personalized Services
Western Union, Engraving, Business Cards, Key Duplication, Leather Name Badges, Watch & Jewelry Repair, and Gift Wrapping

Beauty Salon
Full Service Salon, Manicures & Pedicures. Walk ins welcome, appointment suggested

Barber Shop
Men's cuts. Walk ins welcome.

Tailor Shop
Alterations on uniforms and civilian clothing, Custom Suits
& embroidery

24 Hour Laundromat
Vision Center
Softbank Cellphone Service

Children's Store
Baby Care (diapers, wipes, formula, etc.), Apparel & Shoes,
Navy Pride & Hello Kitty Shops, Nursery Furniture,
Strollers, Car seats.

Home Store
Kitchen Appliances, Bed & Bath, Luggage, Home Storage
& Decor

Home Gallery
Furniture, Mattresses, Home Decor, Rugs & Lamps

USN Hospital Mini Mart
Health & Comfort Items, Snacks & Beverages

Fleet Rec Retail & Services
First Floor
Lockers Club- 24-hour access, Western Union, Laundry/Dry
Cleaning, 24 Hour Laundromat, Barbershop (located outside
of the building)

Second Floor

Uniform Center & Tailor Shop, Activewear & Shoes, GNC & Sports Supplements, Camping & Bicycles, Tactical Gear, Sporting Goods, iRepair Computer & iPhone Repair FadTech Telecom Services

NEX Depot

Office Supplies, Hardware & Power Tools, Catering Supplies, Major Appliances, Home & Office Supplies, Stationery, Furniture & Appliance Special Orders.

Mini Mart/ Gas Station

Food, Snacks & Beverages, Lawn & Garden, Outdoor Furniture & Grills, Pet Food & Supplies, Motorcycle Safety gear, Hardware, Tools, Car Accessories & Drive-thru Car Wash.

Car Care Center

Automotive Repair, Tires, Base Inspection & Propane Tank Refill

Kennel & Grooming Services

Boarding & Grooming

Car Rental & Car Insurance

Car Insurance, Rental Services including Cars, Vans, Trucks, Rug Doctor, AFN Decoder, Insurance & Satellite Dishes Available for purchase.

Dry Cleaners

Pack & Wrap/Laundry

Pack and Wrap for packages, Laundry drop off services

Unaccompanied Baggage/Express Shipment

KITCHEN

- 1-3 Pots & Pans that you use most frequently
- Cooking Utensils (tongs, spatula, large spoon)
- Colander
- Can Opener
- Wine Opener
- Vegetable Peeler
- Cutting board
- Chef's knife
- Flatware (enough for every one for at least one meal)
- Plates
- Cups (something that can stand hot or cold, like Tervis Tumblers for example)
- Coffee Maker, French Press or Hot Water Kettle
- Salt, Pepper, Favorite spices (garlic, oregano, onion powder, etc…)
- Casserole dish (preferably with a lid for easy food storage)
- Tupperware/food storage
- Ziploc bags
- Plastic wrap/Aluminum foil
- Dish towels

- Dish Detergent Pods
- Sponge or scouring pads
- Dish detergent
- Trash Can
- Trash Bags

BATHROOM
- Towels
- Any leftover toiletries
- Bath Mats
- Shower Caddies
- Shower Curtains
- Cleaning Supplies (Toilet bowl brushes, plunger)
- Mini bathroom trash Cans

BEDROOM
- Sheets, blanket and pillow for each bed (Twin and Queens Available for each family member)
- Hangers (enough to hang/organize items each family member will have until HHG furniture arrives)
- Laundry hampers

MISCELLANEOUS
- Paper towels
- Toilet Paper
- Emergency Preparedness Kit
- Laundry detergent
- Dryer Sheets

- Throw pillows/blankets
- Printer
- Printer Paper
- Computer/Laptop
- Bikes & helmets (This will make getting around base a bit easier and less expensive than utilizing taxis)
- Vacuum
- Broom
- Dustpan and brush

CHILDREN
- Extra clothes
- Comfort items
- Extra Diapers
- Formula
- Entertainment (favorite DVDs etc...)
- Extra strollers/gear you were unable to hand carry, but will want those first few days or weeks
- Bikes/scooters

Where to eat/Restaurants

Club Alliance Building 1495 (Next to Main Gate)
- Italian Gardens Restaurant
- C-Street Grille
- Shark's Road House
- Anchor Lounge
CPO Club Building B37

Officers' Club (All Hands) Building 1493

- Kosano Dining Room
- Chopsticks- Asian To-Go
- Kurofune Lounge
- Warehouse Restaurant

CFAY Base Galley (DFAC) Building 1557

MWR Food Court (Building

- Mean Gene's Burgers
- Smash Hit Subs
- Hot Stuff Pizza
- Cinnamon Street- Bakery & Coffee Co.

Chili's Grill & Bar

Starbucks Building 1559 (Across from Main NEX)

Taco Bell Building 1559 (Next to Starbucks, Across from Main NEX)

NEX Food Court Building H20 (Main NEX Building)

- Dunkin' Donuts & Baskin Robbins
- American Grill
- Anthony's Pizza

Main Street Food Court Building G-59

- Subway
- Seattle's Best Coffee
- A&W
- Manchu Wok
- Popeye's Chicken

McDonald's Building 1496

Bayside Food Court Building A-920

- Pizza Hut
- Seattle's Best Coffee
- Subway

ATMS

- Outside of the Navy Exchange Main Store Food Court Outside of the PSD Building
- Pier side (approximately a block from the ship piers) Autoport
- Behind the parking structure across the street from Fleet Theatre

Money can also be exchanged at the Navy Exchange Main Store customer service desk and the cash cage on the second floor of the A club.

What to pack in your bags going with you

First Days Bag

I packed one of these in the event that we were unable to receive our express shipment the day we moved into our apartment. We did end up using it; however, housing is usually willing to work with you if there is an extenuating circumstance. I did this because I knew we would be in transit for several months with schools and other commitments and would be desperate to get out of the Navy Lodge. While this worked out well for us, this may be impractical if you have little ones, as the biggest gift you can give yourself is to travel as light as possible!

- One large versatile pan
- Spatula

- Tongs
- Can Opener
- Wine Opener
- Vegetable peeler
- Various size plastic bags
- 1-2 trash bags
- 1-2 Kitchen towels
- Laundry detergent pods
- Stain Remover
- Dryer sheets
- Quarters
- Reusable collapsible bags
- Towels
- Sheets
- Blankets
- Pillows
- Clean up kit (dish soap, scouring pad, Clorox wipes, cleaning solution)
- Laptop or External hard drive with full back up
- Chargers
- External battery packs
- Rain gear (coat, poncho, rain boots and/or umbrellas)

What to have in your Emergency Kit

- PCS Binder/Folder with all important documents
- Blank Health Certificate from the base veterinarian for air travel with your pet
- Cooking kit

- 1 to 2 day supply of food & water for your entire family Toilet paper
- Paper towels Hygienic wipes
- Disposable plates/bowls and flatware

Self Help List of Things Available

- Loaner Tools Calking gun Face Shield
- Hand Saw, Crosscut Paint Tray with Roller Rake
- Aluminum Stepladder Window Cleaner Floor Polisher
- Hand Spreader Toilet Plunger
- Long Handle Grass Shear Drop Cloth
- Hack Saw Hedge Trimmer Putty Knife
- Steam Vac Cleaner Supplies/Materials Sand Paper
- Door Security Chain Grass Seed
- Interior paint/Touchup Paint 9" Paint Roller Refills
- Tool Kit
- Weather Strip (Window/Door) Waterproof Caulking Compound Doorstop & Door Holder
- Insect Screen Patching Putty 1" Masking Tape Top Soil Fertilizer
- Nails
- Paint Brushes Toilet Seat Weed Killer Full Tour Items
- Dehumidifier
- Step Up Transformer

MWR WIFI Hot Spots

- Officer's Club
- CPO Club- Cove Bar Club Alliance Sports Bar Spectrum Liberty Center
- J.D. Kelly Fleet Rec Center (3rd Floor) CFAY Library
- Green Beach Pool Deck Yokosuka Bowling Center Oksana Park
- Green Bay Marina ITT/Starbucks Outdoor Area

Key: navy.mwr
User Name: mar
Password: YokosukaMWR

You will then be required to open a browser and agree to the terms and conditions to connect.

Gates & Hours of Operation

Main Gate
24/7

Womble Gate
5:00-22:00 daily

Daiei Gate
Monday-Friday 06:00-20:00
Saturday 07:00-08:00 16:30-17:30
Closed on Sundays and Holidays

Useful Apps

Keep In Touch
- Skype iMessage
- WhatsApp Line
- TextNow
- Facebook Messenger

Getting Around
- Google Maps
- Apple Maps
- Google Translate
- Japan Rail

Staying Organized
- Cam Scanner
- DropBox
- iCloud Drive
- Wunderlist
- PocketLife

ABOUT THE AUTHOR

My name is Ciara Skiles. I am a proud military spouse living here in Yokosuka with my husband, Elliott and fur baby, James. In our five years of marriage, we have had a total of four PCS moves, with two of them being overseas. I am a firm believer that as difficult as it is to move as often as we do, it is truly something to be grateful for. I have met so many incredible people in our journeys that have inspired me in ways I could have never expected and also experienced the amazing generosity and hospitality of the military community. My mantra in life is to embrace my community as much as I can, and find my tribe wherever I go because it is much easier to bloom where you are planted when you have people to fill your bucket and provide a little sunshine along the way.

Made in the USA
Middletown, DE
10 December 2019